# Table of Contents

Chicken . . . . . . . . . . . . . . . . 4

Beef & Pork . . . . . . . . . . . . 16

Seafood . . . . . . . . . . . . . . . 28

Vegetables . . . . . . . . . . . . 38

# Chicken Florentine in Minutes

**Makes 4 servings**

3 cups water

1 cup milk

2 tablespoons butter

2 packages (about 4 ounces each) fettuccine Alfredo or stroganoff pasta mix

¼ teaspoon black pepper

1 package (about 10 ounces) refrigerated fully cooked chicken breast strips, cut into ½-inch pieces

4 cups baby spinach, coarsely chopped

¼ cup diced roasted red pepper

¼ cup sour cream

1 Bring water, milk and butter to a boil in large saucepan over medium-high heat. Stir in pasta mix and black pepper. Reduce heat to medium; cook 8 minutes or until pasta is tender, stirring occasionally.

2 Add chicken, spinach and roasted pepper; cook 2 minutes or until heated through. Remove from heat; stir in sour cream.

# Quick Hot and Sour Chicken Soup

## Makes 4 servings

2 cups water

2 cups chicken broth

1 package (about 10 ounces) refrigerated fully cooked chicken breast strips, cut into pieces

1 package (about 7 ounces) chicken-flavored rice and vermicelli mix

1 jalapeño pepper,* minced

2 green onions, chopped

1 tablespoon soy sauce

1 tablespoon lime juice

1 tablespoon minced fresh cilantro

*Jalapeño peppers can sting and irritate the skin, so wear rubber gloves when handling peppers and do not touch your eyes.*

1 Combine water, broth, chicken, rice mix, jalapeño, green onions and soy sauce in large saucepan; bring to a boil over high heat. Reduce heat to low; cover and simmer 20 minutes or until rice is tender, stirring occasionally.

2 Stir in lime juice; sprinkle with cilantro.

# Bow Tie Pasta Bowl

## Makes 4 servings

3  cups reduced-sodium chicken broth

6  ounces uncooked bow tie pasta

⅛  teaspoon red pepper flakes

1½ cups diced cooked chicken

1  medium tomato, seeded and diced

1  cup packed spring greens or spinach, coarsely chopped

3  tablespoons chopped fresh basil

⅛  teaspoon salt

1  cup (4 ounces) shredded mozzarella cheese

2  tablespoons grated Parmesan cheese

1  Bring broth to boil in large saucepan over high heat. Add pasta and red pepper flakes; return to a boil. Reduce heat to medium-low; cover and simmer 10 minutes or until pasta is tender.

2  Add chicken; cook 1 minute. Remove from heat; stir in tomato, greens, basil and salt. Top with mozzarella and Parmesan.

# Mushroom and Chicken Skillet

**Makes 4 servings**

1 pound boneless skinless chicken breasts, cut into bite-size pieces

1 can (about 14 ounces) chicken broth

¼ cup water

2 cups uncooked instant rice

½ teaspoon dried thyme

8 ounces mushrooms, thinly sliced

1 can (10¾ ounces) cream of celery soup, undiluted

Chopped fresh parsley

**1** Combine chicken, broth and water in large skillet; bring to a boil over medium-high heat. Stir in rice and thyme; top with mushrooms. (Do not stir mushrooms into rice.) Cover skillet; turn off heat and let stand 5 minutes.

**2** Stir in soup; cook over low heat 5 minutes or until heated through. Sprinkle with parsley.

# Confetti Chicken Chili

**Makes 5 servings**

2  teaspoons olive oil

1  pound ground chicken
   or turkey

1  large onion, chopped

3½  cups reduced-sodium
   chicken broth

1  can (about 15 ounces)
   Great Northern beans,
   rinsed and drained

2  carrots, chopped

1  medium green bell pepper,
   chopped

2  plum tomatoes, chopped

1  jalapeño pepper,* finely
   chopped (optional)

2  teaspoons chili powder

½  teaspoon ground red pepper

*Jalapeño peppers can sting and irritate the skin, so wear rubber
gloves when handling peppers and do not touch your eyes.*

1  Heat oil in large saucepan over medium heat. Add chicken
   and onion; cook and stir 5 minutes or until chicken is browned.
   Drain fat.

2  Add broth, beans, carrots, bell pepper, tomatoes, jalapeño,
   if desired, chili powder and red pepper; bring to a boil over
   high heat. Reduce heat to low; cover and simmer 15 minutes.

# Chunky Chicken Stew

**Makes 2 servings**

1 teaspoon olive oil

1 small onion, chopped

1 can (about 14 ounces) diced tomatoes

1 cup chicken broth

1 cup thinly sliced carrots

¼ teaspoon salt

⅛ teaspoon black pepper

3 cups sliced kale or baby spinach

1 cup diced cooked chicken breast

1 Heat oil in large saucepan over medium-high heat. Add onion; cook and stir about 5 minutes or until golden brown. Add tomatoes, broth, carrots, salt and pepper; bring to a boil. Reduce heat to medium-low; simmer about 10 minutes or until carrots are tender.

2 Stir in kale and chicken; cook and stir until kale is until wilted.

# Picadillo Tacos

**Makes 2 servings**

6 ounces ground beef

½ cup chopped green bell pepper

½ teaspoon ground cumin

½ teaspoon chili powder

⅛ teaspoon ground cinnamon

½ cup chunky salsa

1 tablespoon golden raisins

4 (6-inch) corn tortillas, warmed

Toppings: shredded lettuce, shredded Cheddar cheese and chopped tomato

1 Combine ground beef, bell pepper, cumin, chili powder and cinnamon in large nonstick skillet; cook and stir over medium heat until beef is browned.

2 Add salsa and raisins; simmer over low heat 5 minutes or until beef is cooked through, stirring occasionally.

3 Divide beef mixture evenly among tortillas; serve with desired toppings.

# Asian Vegetables and Ham

**Makes 4 servings**

2 cups reduced-sodium chicken broth

1 package (16 ounces) frozen stir-fry vegetables

1 teaspoon sesame oil

4 ounces thinly sliced ham, cut into ½-inch squares

2 cups uncooked instant long grain rice

Light soy sauce (optional)

---

**1** Combine broth, frozen vegetables and sesame oil in large saucepan; bring to a boil over high heat.

**2** Remove from heat; stir in ham and rice. Cover and let stand 5 minutes. Serve with soy sauce, if desired.

## Variation

Substitute 12 ounces cooked chicken for the ham.

# All-in-One Burger Stew

**Makes 6 servings**

1  pound lean ground beef

2  cups frozen Italian-style vegetables

1  can (about 14 ounces) diced tomatoes with basil and garlic

1  can (about 14 ounces) beef broth

2½  cups uncooked medium egg noodles

Salt and black pepper

1  Brown beef in large skillet over medium-high heat 6 to 8 minutes, stirring to break up meat. Drain fat.

2  Add frozen vegetables, tomatoes and broth; bring to a boil over high heat.

3  Stir in noodles. Reduce heat to medium; cover and cook 12 to 15 minutes or until vegetables and noodles are tender. Season with salt and pepper.

# Kielbasa & Cabbage Soup

**Makes 8 servings**

1 pound Polish kielbasa, cut into ½-inch cubes

1 package (16 ounces) coleslaw mix (shredded green cabbage and carrots)

3 cans (14½ ounces each) beef broth

1 can (12 ounces) beer or nonalcoholic malt beverage

1 cup water

½ teaspoon caraway seeds

2 cups FRENCH'S® French Fried Onions, divided

Garnish: fresh dill sprigs (optional)

1 Coat 5-quart pot or Dutch oven with nonstick cooking spray. Cook kielbasa over medium-high heat about 5 minutes or until browned. Add coleslaw mix; sauté until tender.

2 Add broth, beer, water, caraway seeds and *1 cup* French Fried Onions; bring to a boil over medium-high heat. Reduce heat to low. Simmer, uncovered, 10 minutes to blend flavors. Spoon soup into serving bowls; top with remaining onions. Garnish with fresh dill sprigs, if desired.

# Swirly Noodle Taco Skillet

**Makes 6 servings**

1  pound ground beef

1  onion, diced (about 1 cup)

1  packet (1.25 ounces) ORTEGA® Taco Seasoning Mix

1  can (7 ounces) ORTEGA® Fire-Roasted Diced Green Chilies

1  jar (16 ounces) ORTEGA® Salsa, any variety

½  pound rotini or fusilli pasta, uncooked

Shredded Cheddar cheese (optional)

**BROWN** ground beef and onion in large skillet over medium-high heat 6 to 8 minutes, stirring to break up meat. Drain fat.

**ADD** taco seasoning mix, chilies, salsa a nd 2 cups water; stir to combine. Add pasta and stir. Reduce heat to low. Cover and cook 12 to 14 minutes or until pasta is cooked through. Serve with cheese.

## Tip

This dish also makes a great taco filling, for ORTEGA® Yellow Corn Taco Shells or soft flour tortillas.

# Italian Sausage and Vegetable Stew

**Makes 6 servings**

1 pound hot or mild Italian sausage links, cut into 1-inch pieces

1 package (16 ounces) frozen vegetable blend, such as onions and bell peppers

2 medium zucchini, sliced

1 can (about 14 ounces) Italian-style diced tomatoes

1 can (4 ounces) sliced mushrooms, drained

4 cloves garlic, minced

1 Brown sausage in large saucepan over medium-high heat 5 minutes, stirring frequently. Drain fat.

2 Add frozen vegetables, zucchini, tomatoes, mushrooms and garlic; bring to a boil. Reduce heat to medium-low; cover and simmer 10 minutes. Uncover; cook 5 to 10 minutes or until thickened slightly.

# Shrimp and Pepper Noodle Bowl

**Makes 4 servings**

4  cups water

2  packages (3 ounces each) shrimp-flavored ramen noodles

8  ounces frozen cooked medium or baby shrimp

1  cup frozen bell pepper strips

¼  cup chopped green onions

1  tablespoon soy sauce

½  teaspoon hot pepper sauce

2  tablespoons chopped fresh cilantro (optional)

**1** Bring water to a boil in large saucepan over high heat. Remove seasoning packets from noodles; set aside. Break up noodles; add to boiling water. Add shrimp and bell pepper; cook 3 minutes.

**2** Add seasoning packets, green onions, soy sauce and hot pepper sauce; cook 1 minute. Sprinkle with cilantro, if desired.

# New Orleans Fish Soup

**Makes 4 servings**

1 can (about 15 ounces) cannellini beans, rinsed and drained

1 can (about 14 ounces) reduced-sodium chicken broth

1 yellow squash, halved lengthwise and sliced (1 cup)

1 tablespoon Cajun seasoning

2 cans (about 14 ounces each) stewed tomatoes

1 pound skinless firm fish fillets, such as grouper, cod or haddock, cut into 1-inch pieces

½ cup sliced green onions

1 teaspoon grated orange peel

1 Combine beans, broth, squash and Cajun seasoning in large saucepan; bring to a boil over high heat.

2 Stir in tomatoes and fish. Reduce heat to medium-low; cover and simmer 3 to 5 minutes or until fish begins to flake when tested with fork. Stir in green onions and orange peel.

# Shrimp & Corn Chowder with Sun-Dried Tomatoes

**Makes 4 servings**

1 can (10¾ ounces)
CAMPBELL'S® Condensed
Cream of Potato Soup

1½ cups half-and-half

2 cups whole kernel corn,
drained

2 tablespoons sun-dried
tomatoes, cut into strips

1 cup small **or** medium peeled
and deveined cooked
shrimp

2 tablespoons chopped fresh
chives

Ground black pepper

---

1 Heat the soup, half-and-half, corn and tomatoes in a 3-quart saucepan over medium heat to a boil. Reduce the heat to low. Cook for 10 minutes.

2 Stir in the shrimp and chives and cook until the mixture is hot and bubbling. Season with the black pepper.

## Tip

For a lighter version, use skim milk
instead of the half-and-half.

# Italian Fish Soup

**Makes 2 servings**

1 cup meatless pasta sauce

¾ cup water

¾ cup reduced-sodium chicken broth

1 teaspoon Italian seasoning

¾ cup uncooked small pasta shells

1½ cups frozen vegetable blend, such as broccoli, carrots and water chestnuts or broccoli, carrots and cauliflower

4 ounces fresh halibut or haddock steak, 1 inch thick, skinned and cut into 1-inch pieces

**1** Combine pasta sauce, water, broth and Italian seasoning in medium saucepan; bring to a boil over high heat. Stir in pasta; return to a boil. Reduce heat to medium-low; cover and simmer 5 minutes.

**2** Add frozen vegetables and fish; return to a boil. Cover and simmer over medium-low heat 4 to 5 minutes or until pasta is tender and fish begins to flake when tested with fork.

# Curried Shrimp and Noodles

**Makes 4 servings**

3  cups water

2  packages (about 1.6 ounces each) instant curry-flavored rice noodle soup mix

1  package (8 ounces) frozen cooked baby shrimp

1  cup frozen bell pepper strips, cut into 1-inch pieces or 1 cup frozen peas

¼  cup chopped green onions

¼  teaspoon salt

¼  teaspoon black pepper

1  to 2 tablespoons lime juice

**1** Bring water to a boil in large saucepan over high heat. Add soup mixes, shrimp, bell pepper, green onions, salt and black pepper; cook 3 to 5 minutes or until noodles are tender, stirring frequently.

**2** Stir in lime juice. Serve immediately.

# Szechuan Vegetable Lo Mein

## Makes 4 servings

2  cans (about 14 ounces each) vegetable broth

2  teaspoons minced garlic

1  teaspoon minced fresh ginger

¼  teaspoon red pepper flakes

1  package (16 ounces) frozen vegetable medley, such as broccoli, carrots, water chestnuts and red bell peppers

1  package (5 ounces) Asian curly noodles or 5 ounces uncooked angel hair pasta, broken in half

3  tablespoons soy sauce

1  tablespoon dark sesame oil

¼  cup thinly sliced green onions

1 Combine broth, garlic, ginger and red pepper flakes in large saucepan; bring to a boil over high heat. Add frozen vegetables and noodles; cover and return to a boil. Reduce heat to medium-low; simmer, uncovered, 5 to 6 minutes or until vegetables and noodles are tender, stirring occasionally.

2 Stir in soy sauce and sesame oil; cook 3 minutes. Stir in green onions just before serving.

## Tip

For a heartier, protein-packed main dish, add 1 package (14 ounces) extra firm tofu, drained and cut into ¾-inch cubes, to the broth mixture with the soy sauce and sesame oil.

# Minestrone Soup

**Makes 4 to 6 servings**

2  cans (about 14 ounces each)
vegetable broth

1  can (28 ounces) crushed
tomatoes in tomato purée

1  can (about 15 ounces) white
beans, rinsed and drained

¾  cup uncooked small shell
pasta

1  package (16 ounces) frozen
vegetable medley, such
as broccoli, green beans,
carrots and red bell
peppers

4  to 6 teaspoons prepared
pesto

1  Combine broth, tomatoes and beans in large saucepan; bring
to a boil over high heat. Stir in pasta; cook 7 minutes.

2  Add frozen vegetables; cook until pasta is tender and vegetables
are heated through.

3  Spoon about 1 teaspoon pesto in center of each serving.

# Rotini with Spinach, Beans and Romano Cheese

**Makes 6 servings**

8 cups fresh spinach, stemmed and leaves torn

1 can (about 15 ounces) cannellini or Great Northern beans, rinsed and drained

½ cup shredded or grated Romano cheese

2 tablespoons olive oil

2 cloves garlic, minced

¼ teaspoon salt

¼ teaspoon black pepper

4 cups hot cooked multigrain or whole wheat rotini

1 Combine spinach, beans, cheese, oil, garlic, salt and pepper in large bowl; mix well.

2 Add hot rotini; toss gently until well blended and spinach is wilted.

## Note

The heat of the cooked rotini will wilt the spinach. If you prefer cooked spinach, steam it briefly before adding it to the rotini with the rest of the ingredients.

# Tex-Mex Black Bean and Corn Stew

**Makes 4 servings**

1 tablespoon canola or vegetable oil

1 small onion, chopped

4 cloves garlic, minced

1 teaspoon chili powder

1 teaspoon ground cumin

1 can (about 15 ounces) black beans, rinsed and drained

1 can (about 14 ounces) fire-roasted diced tomatoes

¾ cup salsa

2 medium zucchini or yellow squash (or 1 of each), cut into ½-inch chunks

1 cup frozen corn

½ cup (2 ounces) shredded Cheddar or pepper jack cheese (optional)

¼ cup chopped fresh cilantro or green onions (optional)

1 Heat oil in large saucepan over medium heat. Add onion; cook and stir 5 minutes or until translucent. Add garlic, chili powder and cumin; cook and stir 1 minute.

2 Add beans, tomatoes, salsa, zucchini and corn; bring to a boil over high heat. Reduce heat to low; cover and simmer 15 minutes or until vegetables are tender. Top with Cheddar and cilantro, if desired..

# Quick Tuscan Bean, Tomato and Spinach Soup

**Makes 4 servings**

2 cans (about 14 ounces each) diced tomatoes with onions

1 can (about 14 ounces) chicken broth

2 teaspoons sugar

2 teaspoons dried basil

¾ teaspoon Worcestershire sauce

1 can (about 15 ounces) small white beans, rinsed and drained

3 ounces baby spinach

1 tablespoon extra virgin olive oil

---

**1** Combine tomatoes, broth, sugar, basil and Worcestershire sauce in large saucepan; bring to a boil over high heat. Reduce heat to low; simmer 10 minutes.

**2** Add beans and spinach; cook 5 minutes or until spinach is tender.

**3** Stir in oil just before serving.

**Vegetables**